Teach Your Children To Read Well

LEVEL 1B: GRADE K-2
STUDENT WORKBOOK

Michael Maloney
Lynne Brearley
Judie Preece

Teach Your Children Well Press

Belleville, Ontario, Canada

Teach Your Children Well
208-210 Front Street, Second Floor
P.O. Box 908, Belleville, Ontario K8N 5B6
Canada

ISBN 1-894595-18-1

LESSON 31

Exercise 1

A		B
hug__	•	• ate
cut__	•	• slope
hop__	•	• cube
slim__	•	• cute
slop__	•	• hope
mad__	•	• slime
cub__	•	• huge
at__	•	• made

Exercise 2

A	B	
1. stop	_g_ ō̲	✓gō
2. ask	__ __ __ __ ◯ __ __	tall
3. summer	__ __ __ __ ◯ __	winter
4. ōpen	__ __ __ __ __	black
5. push	__ ◯ __ __	answer
6. small	__ __ __ __ __	pull
7. white	__ ◯ __ __ __ __	close

 a __ __ __ __ __

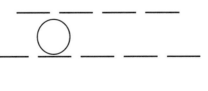

1

spin   hate
five   time   can
plane   spine   hat
plan   tire

— — — — —

— — — —

— — — —

— — — — —   — — — —

— — —

2

Exercise 4

1. Thē pāper plane bēgan to spin and fall down.

2. _____thē_____when it is time.

3. Thē_____cub went into thē pond.

4. _____thē thrēē_____left and _____up thē slope.

5. Wē plāy thē game and hope to win thē gold.

6. A_____plan can cut thē_____.

7. Quit jumping along with that stiff stick.

8. Thē spine is important to kēēp your back stiff.

9. That_____girl is_____.

10. Then hē got mad when thē slop fell.

11. Is hē an_____person?

12. Do not catch thē little ball.

13. After shē left, wē felt sad and down.

Exercise 5

```
w t c i a d m t r
o f t e n e t u c
n p h c o s t r f
i m p o r t a n t
m a r s a i c d q
e d u l n c u b s
v q u i c k b i j
r b o m t l e k c
```

quick ☞ cube ☞
cost ☞ damp ☜
stick ☜ often ☞
turn ☜ cubs ☞
cute ☞ ran ☜
slim ☜
important ☞

LESSON 31

Working Hard	1	2	3	4	5	6	7	8	9	10
Paying Attention	1	2	3	4	5	6	7	8	9	10
Following Instructions	1	2	3	4	5	6	7	8	9	10
Workbook Exercises	1	2	3	4	5	6	7	8	9	10
Fluency Checks	1	2	3	4	5	6	7	8	9	10

TOTAL POINTS: _____

LESSON 32

Exercise 1

Words which follōw thē fīnal e rule		Words which do <u>not</u> follōw thē fīnal e rule
_____	rob	_____
_____	mat	_____
_____	ate	_____
_____	lake	_____
_____	month	_____
_____	white	
	here	
	slim	
	alive	
	cube	

Exercise 2

1. Thē big truck was_____and grēēn.

2. Thē hill was_____.

3. Thē truck_____back down thē

   stēēp_____.

4. It went_____into a_____.

5. A_____was_____at thē

_____of thē_____.

6. Shē got_____ at thē _____ in

thē truck.

7. Shē made thē_____man take her to

thē_____store.

 Exercise 3

wet
pet
pot
not

_____

_____

_____

_____

_____

_____

6

What do you get if your dog falls into a pond?

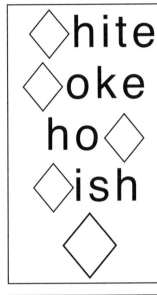

◇hite
◇oke
ho◇
◇ish
◇

tir□
sudd□n
pāp□r
h□lp
□

s○ēēp
○op
di○ch
win○er
○

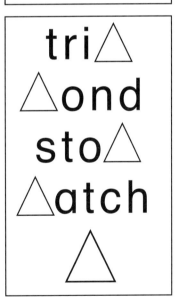

tri△
△ond
sto△
△atch
△

a _____ ◇ □ ○ _____ △ □ ○

Thē truck is grēēn.

A man is standing at thē front of thē truck.

Hē is happy.

A black dog is bēside thē man.

A big red box is on top of thē truck.

There is a patch on one tire of thē truck.

LESSON 32

Working Hard	1	2	3	4	5	6	7	8	9	10
Paying Attention	1	2	3	4	5	6	7	8	9	10
Following Instructions	1	2	3	4	5	6	7	8	9	10
Workbook Exercises	1	2	3	4	5	6	7	8	9	10
Fluency Checks	1	2	3	4	5	6	7	8	9	10

TOTAL POINTS: _____

LESSON 33

Exercise 1

t _ _ th   sl _ _ p   le _ _ er

pu _ _ y   fa _ _   gla _ _

Exercise 2

Aa Bb Cc Dd Ee Ff Gg Hh Ii Jj Kk Ll
Mm Nn Oo Pp Qq Rr Ss Tt Uu Vv Ww Xx Yy Zz

mine   _ _ ◯ _ _
third   _ _ _ _ ◯
came   _ _ _ ◯ _
plate   _ ◯ _ _ _
first   ◯ _ _ _ _
slēēp   _ _ _ _ ◯
enter   _ ◯ _ _ _

Exercise 3

 _ _ _ _ _ _ _

Exercise 4

What is another word for little kids?

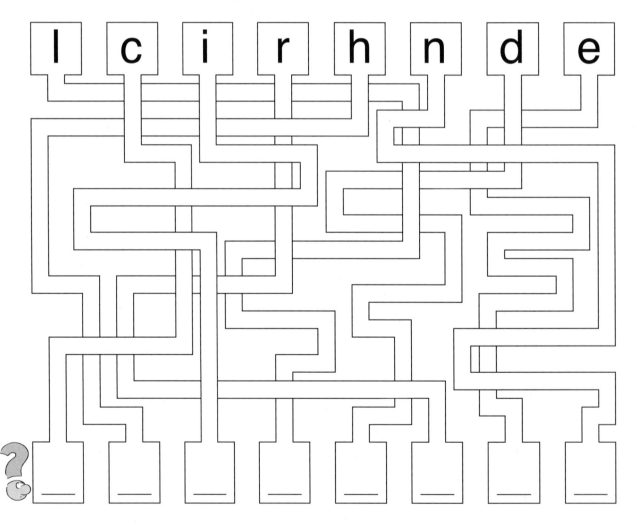

l c i r h n d e

rrr!!

letter	serve	her	fur
under	enter	several	stir
mister	winter	turn	first
number	different		river

not him .... **er**

thē Mississippi .... **er**

more than two .... **er**

not thē same .... **er**

write a _____ .... **er**

on an animal .... **ur**

_____ and Mrs. .... **er**

not second .... **ir**

five is one .... **er**

_____ stick for coffee .... **ir**

offer on a plate .... **er**

not ōver .... **er**

not summer .... **er**

spin around .... **ur**

come into .... **er**

Exercise 6

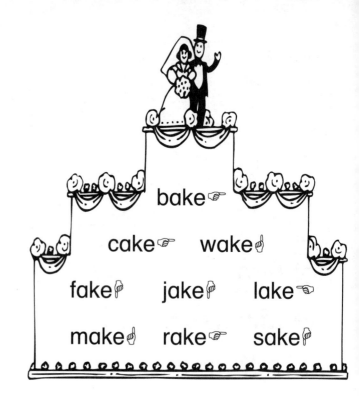

```
c o e k a l
b a k e c f
j r a k e a
a p w a s k
k e n m a e
e k c a k e
m l t r e a
```

bake ☞
cake ☞   wake ☜
fake ☜   jake ☟   lake ☞
make ☜   rake ☞   sake ☜

LESSON 33

Working Hard	1	2	3	4	5	6	7	8	9	10
Paying Attention	1	2	3	4	5	6	7	8	9	10
Following Instructions	1	2	3	4	5	6	7	8	9	10
Workbook Exercises	1	2	3	4	5	6	7	8	9	10
Fluency Checks	1	2	3	4	5	6	7	8	9	10

TOTAL POINTS: _____

LESSON 34

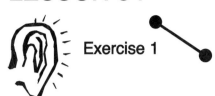 Exercise 1

to •   • mall
bake •   • end
come •   • flȳ
ditch •   • nine
dāy •   • cake
fall •   • full
whȳ •   • some
friend •   • sāy
pull •   • do
mine •   • pitch

 Exercise 2

Z Z

 Exercise 3

1. Today is __ __ __ __ __'__ birthdāy.

2. Shē is asking __ __ __ __ __ friends from

13

her class to come to her __ __ __ __.

3.   They will plāy lots of __ __ __ __ __ and

     have __ __ __ __ .

4.   Thē children bring little __ __ __ __ __ for

     Jenny.

5.   One girl gives her a __ __ __ __ .

6.   In thē box shē fīnds a __ __ __ __ __ __ .

7.   Thē puppy is __ __ __ __ __ and black and

     has big __ __ __ __ .

8.   Thē puppy licks all of thē

     __ __ __ __ __ __ __ __ .

9.   Then thē __ __ __ __ __ licks some

     __ __ __ __ .

10. Now thē puppy is alsō __ __ __ __ __ .

14

Exercise 4

third	mister
happy	catch
enter	plate
bunch	class
serve	perch

c__tch

b__nch

p__rch   s__rv__

th__rd   h__ppy

cl__ss   __nt__r

pl__t__   m__st__r

Exercise 5

1. gas   grēēn   drag   grim

2. nēēd   fēēd   sēēd   shē

3. thin   ram   bin   fin

4. today   mend   send   friend

5. zēbra   buzz   middle   puzzle

6. mȳ   puppy   flȳ   whȳ

Exercise 6

What do you get when you cross a bunny with a puppy?

1.   A letter in **chop** but not in **cop**

2.   A letter in **four** but not in **fur**

3.   A letter in **top** but not in **to**

4.   A letter in **ditch** but not in **itch**

5.   A letter in **ōpen** but not in **pen**

6.   A letter in **wing** but not in **win**

 a ___ ___ ___ ___ ___ ___
      1   2   3   4   5   6

LESSON 34

Working Hard	1	2	3	4	5	6	7	8	9	10
Paying Attention	1	2	3	4	5	6	7	8	9	10
Following Instructions	1	2	3	4	5	6	7	8	9	10
Workbook Exercises	1	2	3	4	5	6	7	8	9	10
Fluency Checks	1	2	3	4	5	6	7	8	9	10

TOTAL POINTS: _____

LESSON 35

Exercise (1)

pin___

slop___

pan___

fir___

plan___

her___

Exercise 2

Z Z Z Z Z Z Z Z Z Z

X Exercise 3

pal   five   cut   cube   shin   time

dim   hope   cute   shelf   puppy   wake

Exercise 4

_____ For her birthdāy Jenny alsō gets a new puppy.

_____ One girl gives her a kite.

_____ Today is Jenny's birthdāy.

_____ Then thē puppy licks some cake that fell from a dish.

_____ Jenny is asking eight friends from her class to come to her home.

_____ Hē licks all of thē children.

Exercise 5

run	run___er	run___ing
plan	plan___er	plan___ing
shop	shop___er	shop___ing
hop	hop___er	hop___ing
set	set___er	set___ing
swim	swim___er	swim___ing
flip	flip___er	flip___ing

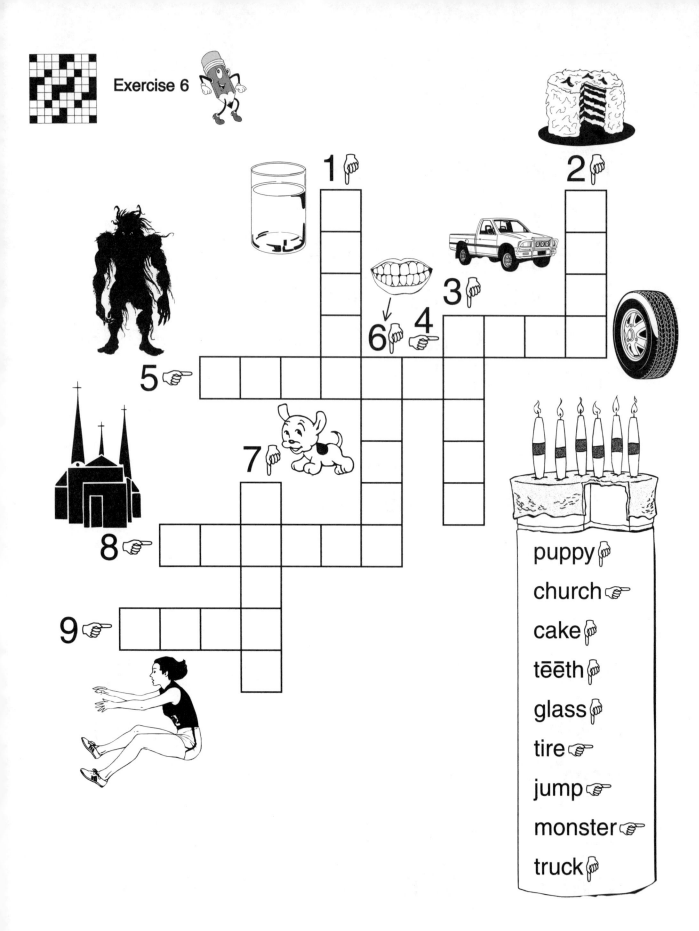

puppy
church
cake
tēēth
glass
tire
jump
monster
truck

Exercise 7

This man has a mask ōver his eyes.

Hē has flippers on his fēēt.

Hē is standing on sand.

Thē sun is shining in thē skȳ.

Thē man is gōing in thē lake for a swim.

Exercise 8 X

What thing has fēēt like flippers?

z z a z f z z z r z o z z g z z

___ ___ ___ ___

Exercise 9

What is another name
for a dīver?

 a fr__gm__n

LESSON 35

Working Hard	1	2	3	4	5	6	7	8	9	10
Paying Attention	1	2	3	4	5	6	7	8	9	10
Following Instructions	1	2	3	4	5	6	7	8	9	10
Workbook Exercises	1	2	3	4	5	6	7	8	9	10
Fluency Checks	1	2	3	4	5	6	7	8	9	10

TOTAL POINTS: _____

LESSON 36

 Exercise 1

happen   catch   angry   gather
ship   sank   problem   hungry

 Exercise 2

Put the letter ȳ in the pan to make it frȳ.

Can you take a ȳ and make it . . .

flȳ	crȳ
sāy bȳe	in thē skȳ

1. otobtm _ _ _ O _ _ bottle

2. gryhru _ O _ _ _ _ lesson

3. selnos _ _ _ _ _ O problem

4. kȳs _ _ _ mūsic

5. ryagn _ O _ _ _ skȳ

6. smcūi _ _ _ _ _ ladder

7. rbmpelo _ _ _ _ _ O _ hungry

8. wsam _ _ _ _ angry

9. etotbl _ _ _ _ O _ swam

10. aedrdl _ _ _ _ _ _ bottom

 _ _ _ _ _ _ _ _

h◇pping
b◇ttle
pr◇blem
b◇tt◇m
◇

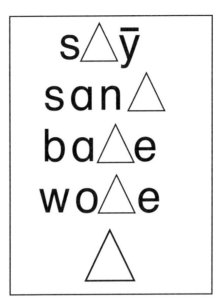

s△ȳ
san△
ba△e
wo△e
△

bun☐h
☐rȳ
☐lass
pi☐ni☐
☐

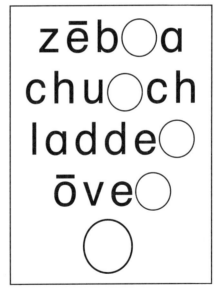

zēb◯a
chu◯ch
ladde◯
ōve◯
◯

◯　◇　☐　△

mūsic

1. __ __iet

2. r__ __ __

3. so__ __

4. __ __rēē

5. __ __ēēl

6. __ __ildren

1. _____   2. _____

3. _____   4. _____

5. _____   6. _____

Exercise 6

buzz

fuzz

LESSON 36

Working Hard	1	2	3	4	5	6	7	8	9	10
Paying Attention	1	2	3	4	5	6	7	8	9	10
Following Instructions	1	2	3	4	5	6	7	8	9	10
Workbook Exercises	1	2	3	4	5	6	7	8	9	10
Fluency Checks	1	2	3	4	5	6	7	8	9	10

TOTAL POINTS: _____

LESSON 37

Exercise 1

e̅a ___ ___ ___ ___ ___

ou ___ ___ ___ ___ ___

ai ___ ___ ___ ___ ___

Exercise 2

loud	train	str e̅am	tail	m e̅at
our	rain	e̅at	sail	afraid
b e̅ast	house	aim	sound	dr e̅am

e̅a	ou	ai
_____	_____	_____
_____	_____	_____
_____	_____	_____
_____	_____	_____
_____	_____	_____

Exercise 3

Z Z Z Z Z Z Z Z

 **Exercise**

1. A se͞a monster came from_____.

   a) the͞ bottom of the͞ lake.

   b) the͞ top of the͞ se͞a.

   c) the͞ bottom of the͞ se͞a.

2. The͞ big be͞ast said, "I will not e͞at _____

   any more."

   a) monsters

   b) fish fins

   c) fish

3. "I ne͞e͞d some re͞al _____.

   a) me͞at to e͞at."

   b) stre͞am to swim."

   c) trout to e͞at."

4. Thē sēā monster has big _____.

      a) grēēn mēāt.

      b) white tēēth.

      c) brown bottles.

5. Thē sēā monster is_____
_____.

      a) grēēn, red and white.

      b) grēēn and black.

      c) grēēn and brown and red.

6. Thē big bēāst swam up a strēām to _____
_____.

      a) thē gates of thē sēā.

      b) thē gates of thē strēām.

      c) thē gates of thē town.

7. "I will trȳ to catch _____.

      a) some children."

      b) Ēdith."

      c) sēā monsters."

8. But thē children can sēē thē monster's_____

    _____.

       a) big tēēth.

       b) one red eye.

       c) long tail.

9. Thē monster made a _____.

       a) long jump.

       b) loud sound.

       c) mēān scrēām.

Exercise 5

Thē sēā monster is

   red and brown.

Thē sēā monster has

   big white tēēth.

Thē sēā monster has

   a long grēēn tail.

Thē sēā monster has

   one big red eye.

 **Exercise 6**

Where do sēā monsters slēēp?

__ __ __ __ __ __ __ __

j o x b u f s

__ __ __ __

c f e t

LESSON 38

 Exercise 1

1. A _____ monster came from thē _____.

2. Thē big _____ swam up a _____ to thē _____ of thē little _____ .

3. Hē is a _____ _____ monster.

4. Thē monster does not _____ thē _____.

5. Hē is _____ and _____.

6. Hē nēēds to find _____ to _____.

 Exercise 2

slēēp •	• scrēam
cast •	• found
house •	• bat
kick •	• dug
sat •	• took
bug •	• sick
trout •	• stēēp
hook •	• mast
drēam •	• about
ground •	• mouse

Exercise 3

th__ __ __

ch__ __ __

__ __ __ck

__ __ __ēa__

__ing

wh__ __ __

__ __ir

__ai__

__ __ou__ __

__ __tch

qu__ __ __

__ol__

__ __ __ __er

__ur

__or__ __ __

__ __al__

r_
ca_
st_
tru_
_ink
_ore
scr_m
gr_nd
moth_
f_est
_ēēn
sm_l
_ite
t_d
s_l
f_

ēach again   sail   nēar ground afraid

out against   yēar found count   mēan

spēak rēad   round wait   pain   about

ou	ai	ēa
_____	_____	_____
_____	_____	_____
_____	_____	_____
_____	_____	_____
_____	_____	_____
_____	_____	_____

 **Exercise 5**

ground ◯ _ _ _ _ _

count _ _ _ ◯ _

wave _ _ _ _

around ◯ _ _ _ _ _

ēach _ _ _ _ _

lēave ◯ _ _ _ _

rēach _ _ _ _ _

yēar ◯ _ _ _

Thē big mēan sēa monster is hungry and _____ .

 _ _ _ _ _ _

36

Exercise 6

What is a mouse's fāvorite game?

(Hide and squeak)

What is a sink's fāvorite game?

(Hide and leak)

What is a robber's fāvorite game?

(Hide and sneak)

What is a plāyground's fāvorite game?

(Slide and seek)

LESSON 38

Working Hard	1	2	3	4	5	6	7	8	9	10
Paying Attention	1	2	3	4	5	6	7	8	9	10
Following Instructions	1	2	3	4	5	6	7	8	9	10
Workbook Exercises	1	2	3	4	5	6	7	8	9	10
Fluency Checks	1	2	3	4	5	6	7	8	9	10

TOTAL POINTS: _____

LESSON 39

Exercise 1

ar _____ _____ _____ _____ _____

oi _____ _____ _____ _____ _____

oy _____ _____ _____ _____ _____

oo _____ _____ _____ _____ _____

Exercise 2

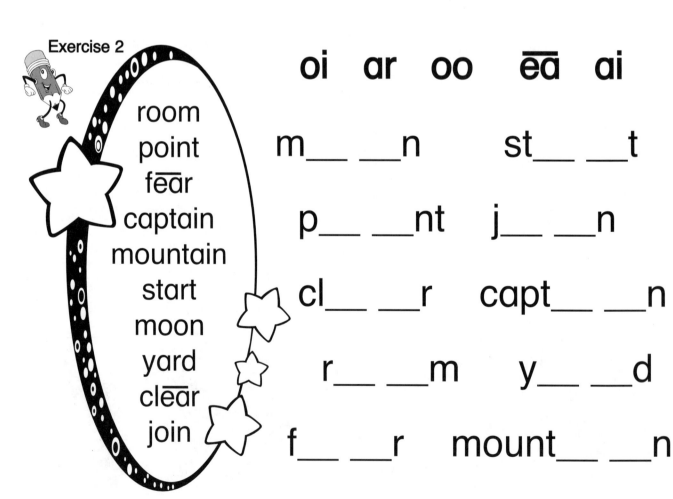

oi ar oo e̅a̅ ai

room
point
fe̅a̅r
captain
mountain
start
moon
yard
cle̅a̅r
join

m__ __n   st__ __t

p__ __nt   j__ __n

cl__ __r   capt__ __n

r__ __m   y__ __d

f__ __r   mount__ __n

Exercise 3

1. Th__ m__ __n s__ __ m__nst__r w__nts t__ __ __t th__ l__ttl__ ch__ldr__n.

2. But thē children sēē thē monster and run home.

3. Thē sēā monster dives into thē sēā.

4. Hē is hungry and angry.

   Hē wants to ēāt mēāt not trout.

5. Wh__n th__ sh__p's m__t__s s__ __ th__ m__nst__r, th__y __r__ __fr__ __d.

6. Now thē captain of thē ship is brave. Hē hits thē monster with a paddle.

7. But thē sēā monster makes a hole in thē ship. Thē ship is sinking. And thē monster is waiting.

Exercise 4 Make a mountain out of a mole hill!

mountain

_____ _____ _____ _____ _____

_____ _____ _____ _____ _____

Exercise 5

a	b	c	d	e	f	g	h	i	k
5	3	8	14	17	16	10	11	9	7
l	m	n	o	p	r	s	t	u	w
1	19	12	4	13	20	2	6	18	15

1. Which sailor are mōst fish afraid of?

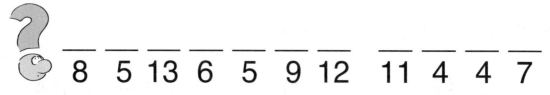

___ ___ ___ ___ ___ ___ ___ ___ ___ ___ ___
 8   5 13   6   5   9 12   11   4   4   7

2. Which dēēp sēā crēātures crȳ thē mōst?

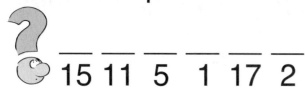

___ ___ ___ ___ ___ ___
15 11   5   1 17   2

40

3. Which dēēp sēā crēātures are thē mōst fāmous?

 __ __ __ __ __ __ __ __
2 6 5 20 16 9 2 11

4. What is a sēā monster's fāvorite food?

 __ __ __ __ __ __ __ __ __ __ __ __
16 9 2 11   5 12 14   2 11 9 13 2

LESSON 39

Working Hard	1	2	3	4	5	6	7	8	9	10
Paying Attention	1	2	3	4	5	6	7	8	9	10
Following Instructions	1	2	3	4	5	6	7	8	9	10
Workbook Exercises	1	2	3	4	5	6	7	8	9	10
Fluency Checks	1	2	3	4	5	6	7	8	9	10

TOTAL POINTS: _____

LESSON 40

  Exercise 1

1. What does thē mēan sēa monster make in thē sailing ship?

   Thē mēan sēa monster makes _____

   _____.

2. Who is in thē sēa?

   A _____ is in thē sēa.

3. What did thē monster sāy to him?

   Thē monster said, "_____

   _____ ."

4. What does thē monster like a lot better than mēat?

   Hē likes _____ a lot better than mēat.

5. Is thē monster mēan now?

   _____

6. How is hē now?

_____

1. star   part   ēar   jar

2. oil   toy   boy   hole

3. fēar   captain   cool   clēar

4. moon   yard   loon   soon

5. hair   without   ground   count

6. wave   hole   ēach   brave

Exercise 3

r m t a m s

a o l l c d

j k i b o y

o n o i s e

i y o t m k

n p o i n t

e r n a i n

oil   boy
join   noise
toy   point

Exercise 4

au ___ ___ ___ ___

aw ___ ___ ___

ould _____ _____ _____

Exercise 5

food	soon	saw	could	bēcause
straw	would	law	should	awful
room	jaw	cool	too	paw

oo	au/aw	ould
_____	_____	_____
_____	_____	_____
_____	_____	_____
_____	_____	_____
_____	_____	
	_____	
	_____	

Exercise 6

○pēak
again○t
hou○e
him○elf
○

wit◇out
◇ungry
◇ard
mout◇
◇

w□uld
b□□t
j□y
r□und
□

r⬡ad
l⬡av⬡
wav⬡
nois⬡
⬡

coo△
awfu△
fau△t
bott△e
△

When does Mrs. Claus mend Santa's socks?

When they have

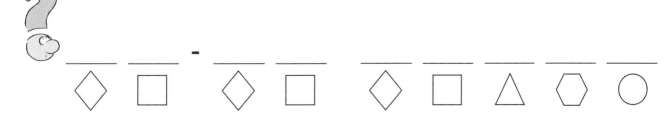

___ ___ - ___ ___   ___ ___ ___ ___ ___

◇ □   ◇ □   ◇ □ △ ⬡ ○

45

LESSON 40

Working Hard	1	2	3	4	5	6	7	8	9	10
Paying Attention	1	2	3	4	5	6	7	8	9	10
Following Instructions	1	2	3	4	5	6	7	8	9	10
Workbook Exercises	1	2	3	4	5	6	7	8	9	10
Fluency Checks	1	2	3	4	5	6	7	8	9	10

TOTAL POINTS: _____

LESSON 41

Exercise 1

start •   • about

skȳ •   • already

paw •   • would

fēar •   • might

head •   • straw

could •   • jar

high •   • gēar

oil •   • cool

moon •   • noise

mouth •   • drȳ

Exercise 2

c = sēē	8 = ate	t = tēā
y = whȳ	= can	 = I
u = you	2 = to, too	r = are

1.   c u.

_____

47

2. r u a good boy?

_____

3. u tell mē y u r sad?

_____

4. c u 8 thē awful

_____

mēat.

_____

5. r u 2 cool 2 gō 2

_____

school?

_____

6. 🥫u tell mē y u like t?

_____

Exercise 3

igh _____   _____   _____   _____

ea _____   _____   _____   _____

Exercise 4

1. Where does Jack live?

   Jack lives_____in a forest.

2. What kīnd of trēēs are in thē forest?

   This forest has lots of_____.

3. Where is thē forest?

   It is on_____.

4. Whȳ can Jack not gō to school?

   It is_____.

5. What does Jack's father do ēach dāy?

   Ēach dāy Jack's father_____

   _____to thē saw mill.

6. What did Jack fīnd one dāy?

   One dāy Jack found_____

   _____.

7. What did they do with thē hurt bear cub?

   They took_____

   _____.

8. Whȳ can Jack not tell his father what is in

   thē book?

   Jack can not tell bēcause hē_____.

X Exercise 5

cabin	pine	trēēs	side	gō	far
cuts	logs	paw	wē	home	first
them	take	sāy	tell	mill	cub

Exercise 6a All right, already!

already

_____ _____ _____ _____ _____

_____ _____ _____ _____ _____

Exercise 6b

dēar   _ _ _ _

lard   _ _ _ _

dēal   _ _ _ _

lead   _ _ _ _

lāy   _ _ _

Exercise 7

What kind of
animal can jump
higher than a house?

(Any kind of animal.
A house can't jump!)

LESSON 41

Working Hard	1	2	3	4	5	6	7	8	9	10
Paying Attention	1	2	3	4	5	6	7	8	9	10
Following Instructions	1	2	3	4	5	6	7	8	9	10
Workbook Exercises	1	2	3	4	5	6	7	8	9	10
Fluency Checks	1	2	3	4	5	6	7	8	9	10

TOTAL POINTS: _____

LESSON 42

Exercise 1

What do little whales learn in school?

1. A letter in **read** but not in **red**.

2. A letter in **bright** but not in **right**.

3. A letter in **scrēam** but not in **crēam**.

4. A letter in **quiet** but not in **quit**.

5. A letter in **mēat** but not in **met**.

6. A letter in **shopping** but not in **hopping**.

They learn their

___, ___, ___ ___ ___ ___.

  1   2   3   4   5   6

Exercise 2   True   False?

1. Jack lives in a house in a small town. _____

2. Jack can't gō to school bēcause it is too far awāy. _____

3. Jack's father cuts logs every dāy. _____

4. One dāy Jack found a hurt mountain cat. _____

5. They found out what to do in thē first-aid book.

_____

6. Jack read thē big first aid book all bȳ himself.

_____

Exercise 3

1. What did Jack fīnd in thē pine forest?

One bright morning Jack found_____

_____ in thē pine forest.

2. Whȳ did Jack and his dad take it back to their cabin?

Hē and his dad got it back to their warm

cabin_____.

54

3. Jack got thē first-aid book but what could Jack not do?

   Jack could not_____.

4. What did Jack's father do first?

   His dad said, "First I will_____

   _____thē bear cub."

5. What did hē sāy to Jack after hē did this?

   Hē said, "Then I will start_____

   _____."

6. When would Jack and his father work?

   Jack and his dad would work_____

   _____for one hour.

7. What would Jack's dad tēach him first?

   First hē would tēach Jack _____,

   then hē would shōw him how to_____

   _____.

Exercise 4

Make something out of nothing!

nothing

_____ _____ _____ _____ _____

_____ _____ _____

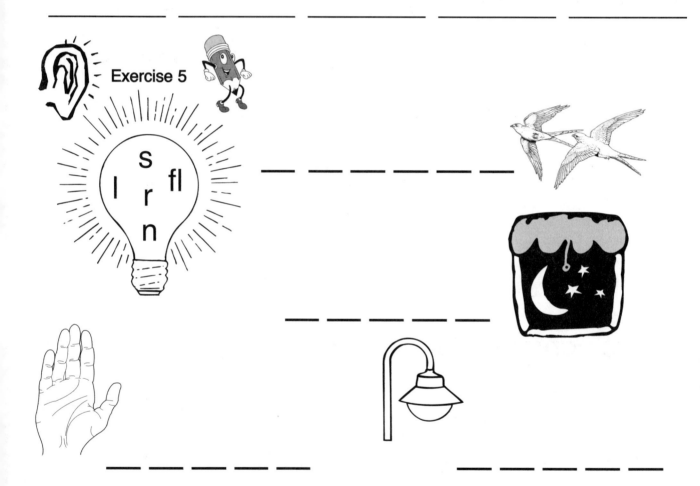

Exercise 5

s
l   fl
r
n

56

Exercise 6

1. dray   ◯ _ _ _ _

2. odof   _ _ ◯ _

3. cqiuk   _ ◯ _ _ _

4. rsosca   _ _ ◯ _ _ _

5. rhotn   ◯ _ _ _ _

6. wpa   _ ◯ _

7. yman   ◯ _ _ _

8. meta   _ ◯ _ _

paw
quick
across
yard
north
tēam
many
food

_ _ _ _   _ _ _ _
1   2   3   4   5   6   7   8

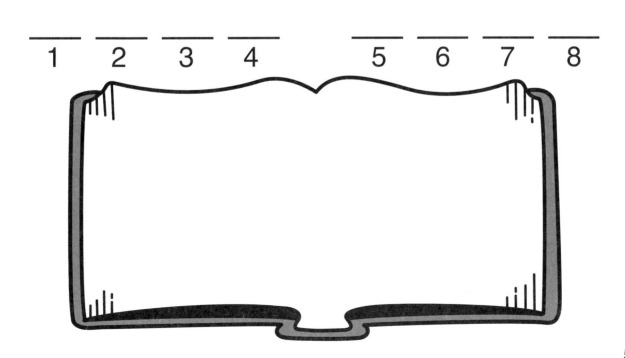

LESSON 42

Working Hard	1	2	3	4	5	6	7	8	9	10
Paying Attention	1	2	3	4	5	6	7	8	9	10
Following Instructions	1	2	3	4	5	6	7	8	9	10
Workbook Exercises	1	2	3	4	5	6	7	8	9	10
Fluency Checks	1	2	3	4	5	6	7	8	9	10

TOTAL POINTS: _____

LESSON 43

Exercise 1

A	B
run_____	set_____
plan_____	swim_____
hot____	get_____
shop____	run_____

Exercise 2

ēa ? ea

1. gear

   clear _____

   leader

2. spread

   dead _____

   head

3. speak

   leave _____

   fear

4. bear

   already _____

   steady

cabin   brave   tunnel   fake   smoke   care

mark   plate   buzz   dinner   silver   wave

bottle   luck   smell   hole   damp   swam

 Exercise 4

_____His father said, "Wē will take him home
and fix his paw."

_____Jack said to his father, "I can't tell you what
is in thē book bēcause I can't rēad."

_____One dāy in thē forest Jack found a bear
cub that had hurt its paw.

_____They got out thē big book on first aid to
fīnd out what to do.

_____His father said, "I will tēach you how to
rēad."

Exercise 5

1. Jack and his father were āble to help thē

   _____ with thē _____ paw to get _____ .

2. Soon Jack bēgan to _____ out words.

3. Soon Jack could _____ .

4. Jack's father said, "You are _____

   _____ ."

5. "Soon you will bē āble to rēad _____

   as _____ as you can _____ ."

6. Jack's father was _____ .

7. In a little while Jack could rēad _____ ,

   ēven thē _____ book.

61

Exercise 6 X b̶ g̶ h j̶ k

What does a bear get if he rubs his paws on a bēach?

hksbjakgnhdbhkygcjlhgakhjwbgsj

_ _ _ _ _

_ _ _ _ _

LESSON 43

Working Hard	1	2	3	4	5	6	7	8	9	10
Paying Attention	1	2	3	4	5	6	7	8	9	10
Following Instructions	1	2	3	4	5	6	7	8	9	10
Workbook Exercises	1	2	3	4	5	6	7	8	9	10
Fluency Checks	1	2	3	4	5	6	7	8	9	10

TOTAL POINTS: _____

LESSON 44

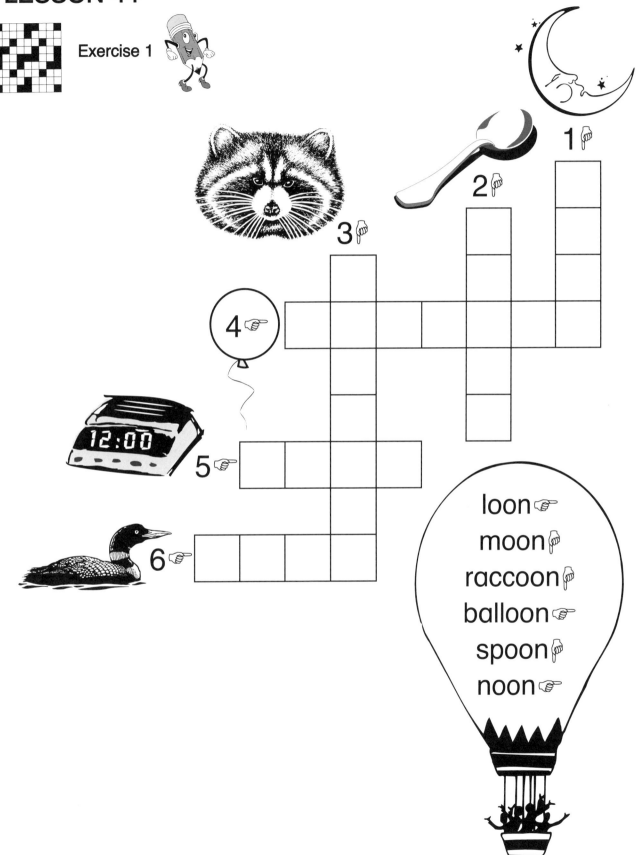

Exercise 1

loon ☞
moon ☞
raccoon ☞
balloon ☞
spoon ☞
noon ☞

Exercise 2

wa _____

g i,e _____

c i,e _____

X **Exercise** ③

(wa)	g̶ i,e̶	□ c i,e
clēan	wash	camping	certain
what	city	water	straight
ginger	cabin	taught	nice
large	forgot	cartoon	chānge

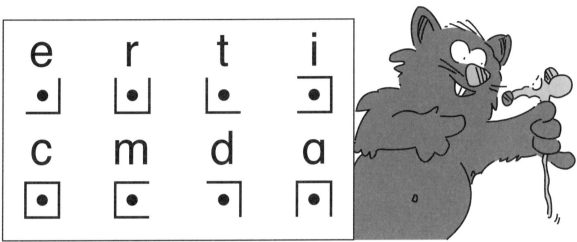

e	r	t	i
c	m	d	a

What is a cat's
fāvorite dessert?

What is a cat's
fāvorite drink?

Exercise 5

1. How do Mark and Jane fēēl?

   Mark and Jane_____.

2. Where are Mark and Jane gōing?

   _____

   _____.

3. What do all of them have?

   They all have_____

   _____.

4. What do they make for dinner?

   _____

   _____.

5. What smells thē food?

   A_____ smells thē

   food from dinner.

6. How does this animal hurt its paw?

   It_____

   _____.

7. Whȳ is thē family afraid?

They look out of thē tent and_____

_____.

Exercise 6

high
sight
act
noon
example
drēam
bēans

LESSON 44

Working Hard	1	2	3	4	5	6	7	8	9	10
Paying Attention	1	2	3	4	5	6	7	8	9	10
Following Instructions	1	2	3	4	5	6	7	8	9	10
Workbook Exercises	1	2	3	4	5	6	7	8	9	10
Fluency Checks	1	2	3	4	5	6	7	8	9	10

TOTAL POINTS: _____

LESSON 45

Exercise 1

100

tent☞ raccoon☜
balloon☞ hundred☜
aslēēp☞ bear☞
paw☜ star☜
mouth☞

Exercise 2

1. What did father sāy to his family?

   Father said, "_____" in a quiet

   voice.

2. What four things did thē bear do?

   Thē bear_____thē fire.

   Then hē_____his paw.

   Hē came ōver to thē tent and_____

   some more.

   Sō hē_____and_____into

   thē woods.

3. Where did thē family gō when they were

   sure thē bear was gone?

   They_____.

4. What did they do after a while?

    They_____

    _____.

5. How did they fēēl there?

    They_____.

6. Did thē bear rēturn?

    _____.

 **Exercise 3**

| sight | voice | two | dead | drift |
| bright | nice | grew | head | dānger |

| move | read | through | gone | plain |
| above | lēād | flew | done | tēam |

| out | hēāl | ocean | appēār |
| shout | learn | climb | here |

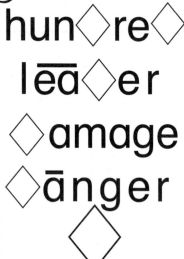

hun◇re◇
lēa◇er
◇amage
◇ānger
◇

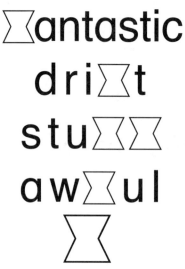

⊠antastic
dri⊠t
stu⊠⊠
aw⊠ul
⊠

ci◯y
◯en◯
sal◯
airpor◯
◯

b☐ans
dang☐r
sist☐r
nic☐
☐

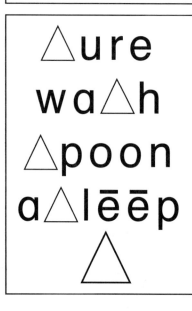

△ure
wa△h
△poon
a△lēēp
△

so⬡th
sho⬡ld
fa⬡lt
co⬡nt
⬡

What did thē teddy bear sāy when hē
was offered dessert?

No, thanks. I'm

____ ____ ____ ____ ____ ____ ____
△   ◯   ⬡   ⊠   ⊠   ☐   ◇

72

LESSON 45

Working Hard	1	2	3	4	5	6	7	8	9	10
Paying Attention	1	2	3	4	5	6	7	8	9	10
Following Instructions	1	2	3	4	5	6	7	8	9	10
Workbook Exercises	1	2	3	4	5	6	7	8	9	10
Fluency Checks	1	2	3	4	5	6	7	8	9	10

TOTAL POINTS: _____

LESSON 46

 Exercise 1

1. Carla is a _____ .

2. Shē sails her boat_____.

3. Sometimes Carla is very_____and

    sometimes very_____.

4. When there is nō wind, shē _____for a

    long time in thē middle of thē ocean.

5. Once thē_____ of her boat was_____

    bȳ a great_____.

6. Her_____got into port.

7. Shē spent a_____fixing thē_____.

8. Carla falls_____.

9. Soon shē would bē in great_____.

 Exercise 2

certain	bored	damage	dēar
wait	bēlōw	bunk	huge
port	watch	page	against
true	curl	brōken	ocean

 Exercise 3

oa _____ _____ _____ _____ _____

 Exercise 4

a b e g o a t
c o a t r a m
c a n a o m o
o t r o a r a
a b f l o a t
m x r a l a e

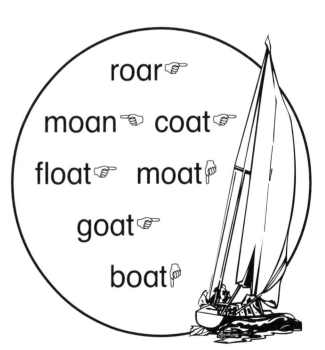

roar☞
moan☞ coat☞
float☞ moat☜
goat☞
boat☟

Exercise 5

What is thē world's slōwest boat?

 a __ __ __ __ __

boat

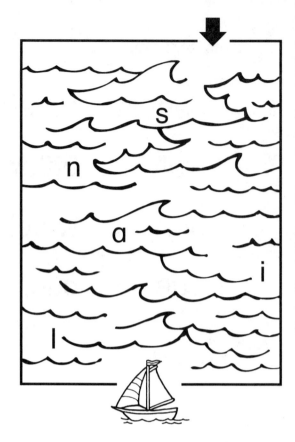

How do you mail a boat?

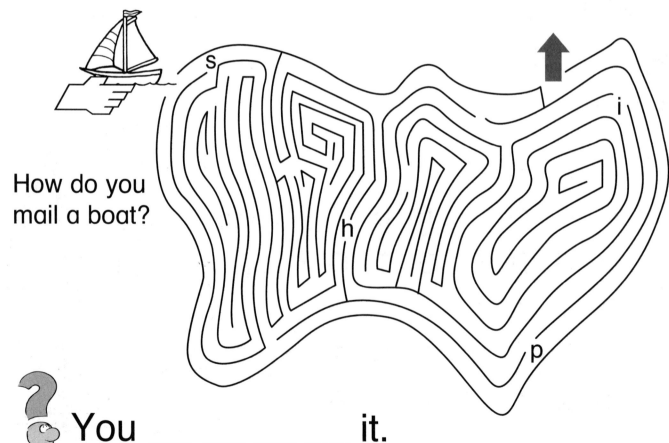

You __ __ __ __ it.

LESSON 46

Working Hard	1	2	3	4	5	6	7	8	9	10
Paying Attention	1	2	3	4	5	6	7	8	9	10
Following Instructions	1	2	3	4	5	6	7	8	9	10
Workbook Exercises	1	2	3	4	5	6	7	8	9	10
Fluency Checks	1	2	3	4	5	6	7	8	9	10

TOTAL POINTS: _____

LESSON 47

Exercise 1

knēē _____ _____ _____

ly _____ _____ _____ _____ _____

Exercise 2

care •   • blue

coat •   • fault

door •   • float

fēar •   • floor

salt •   • lōw

search •   • nēar

straw •   • perch

true •   • raw

thrōw •   • stare

lāy •   • pāy

Exercise 3

1. What was Carla doing at thē bēginning of this story?

    Carla was_____of

    her sloop.

2. What did Carla not knōw?

    Shē did not knōw that shē_____

    _____.

3. How was thē boat sailing?

    It was gōing_____.

4. What was floating in thē water not far ahead?

    Not far ahead a_____ was

    floating in thē water.

5. What was thē container full of?

    It was full of_____

    _____.

6. What happened to Carla when thē large container hit

thē sloop?

Carla was_____

_____.

7. What happened to thē sloop as thē water poured in?

Thē sloop_____ .

Exercise 4

Carla's sloop is blue.
Thē front sail is white with two red stripes across it.
Thē ocean is dark blue.
There is one big grāy cloud in thē skȳ bēhĭnd thē boat.
There is a large container floating in thē water in front of
thē boat.

80

Exercise 5 X

What do you call a fish with two legs?

lytlywlylyolyklynlyly ē lyēlylyflylyilyslylyhly

a _____ _____ - _____ _____ _____

_____ _____ _____ _____ °○

LESSON 47

Working Hard	1	2	3	4	5	6	7	8	9	10
Paying Attention	1	2	3	4	5	6	7	8	9	10
Following Instructions	1	2	3	4	5	6	7	8	9	10
Workbook Exercises	1	2	3	4	5	6	7	8	9	10
Fluency Checks	1	2	3	4	5	6	7	8	9	10

TOTAL POINTS: _____

LESSON 48

Exercise 1

er   ing

shop _____   _____

shut _____   _____

fit   _____   _____

spot _____   _____

plan _____   _____

 Exercise 2

binocūlars

bar __ __ __   in __ __ __

sin __ __ __   an __ __ __

run __ __ __   lob __ __ __

kn

knife

knēē

knock

knōw

ly

quickly

dēēply

ōnly

hardly

Words with vowels that sāy their name		Words with vowels that dōn't sāy their name
	under	
	face	
_____	huge	_____
	rubber	
_____	sunk	_____
	wide	
_____	place	_____
	deck	
_____	life	_____
	prōpane	
_____		_____
_____		_____
_____		_____

Exercise 5

_____ Shē curls up in her bunk and falls aslēēp.

_____ Thē sloop slōwly bēgins to sink.

_____ Carla is a sailor.

_____ A large container hits Carla's sloop.

_____ Carla is sailing southwest under a full moon.

_____ Carla is knocked out bȳ thē crash.

Exercise 6

1. When did Carla wake up?

    Carla woke up_____

    _____.

2. List five things that shē grabbed.

    _____   _____

    _____   _____

    _____

3. What did Carla put into thē water?

She got thē_____

_____.

4. Thē sloop bēgan to slip under thē water.

5. Carla climbed into thē raft and cut it freē from thē boat.

6. Then shē sat there, bobbing about in a huge ocean.

   Carla stared at thē place where her sloop had sunk.

7. Here is Carla in thē rubber raft.

   Draw in her face to shōw what shē was doing at thē

   end of thē story.

LESSON 48

Working Hard	1	2	3	4	5	6	7	8	9	10
Paying Attention	1	2	3	4	5	6	7	8	9	10
Following Instructions	1	2	3	4	5	6	7	8	9	10
Workbook Exercises	1	2	3	4	5	6	7	8	9	10
Fluency Checks	1	2	3	4	5	6	7	8	9	10

TOTAL POINTS: _____

LESSON 49

Exercise 1

1. Carla was on a rubber __ __ __ __. (ftra)

2. When shē looked ōver thē edge shē could sēē ōnly

    miles and miles of __ __ __ __ __ (ptmye)

    __ __ __ __ __ (aeocn).

3. Some __ __ __ __ __ __ __ __ (hpidnsol) swam

    around thē raft.

4. They sēēmed to want to __ __ __ __ . (ylāp)

5. Carla __ __ __ __ __ __ __ (nendcas) thē ocean with

    her __ __ __ __ __ __ __ __ __ __ . (ncoibalrūs)

6. Shē saw __ __ __ __ __ __ __ . (ihntgon)

7. Shē drifted for __ __ __ __ __ (ēhērt) dāys and nights.

8. When a large ship appēāred Carla fired a

    __ __ __ __ __ . (elfra)

9. Thē crew dropped a rope __ __ __ __ __ __ . (dedral)

10. An __ __ __ __ __ __ __ __ (anlperia) saw some stuff

    floating.

11. Carla was soon back on __ __ __ (rȳd) land and soon

    had a new __ __ __ __ __ . (osopl)

Exercise 2

Fun with Words

What is this word?   mt

Print it out in full.   e__p__y

Exercise 3

Māke ten new words from thē letters in thē word

phōtōgraph

_____   _____   _____   _____

_____   _____   _____   _____

_____   _____

Exercise 4

phōtōgraph

_____ _____

_____ _____

Exercise 5

How are cars and elephants alike?

1. A letter in tent but not in ten.

2. A letter in roar but not in oar.

3. A letter in house but not in hose.

4. A letter in pine but not in pie.

5. A letter in sunk but not in sun.

6. A letter in sport but not in port.

 They bōth have __ __ __ __ __ __
  1 2 3 4 5 6

LESSON 49

Working Hard	1	2	3	4	5	6	7	8	9	10
Paying Attention	1	2	3	4	5	6	7	8	9	10
Following Instructions	1	2	3	4	5	6	7	8	9	10
Workbook Exercises	1	2	3	4	5	6	7	8	9	10
Fluency Checks	1	2	3	4	5	6	7	8	9	10

TOTAL POINTS: _____

LESSON 50

Exercise (1)

do	what	pīlot	gravity
tēam	space	lāter	hard
place	told	hōbō	patches
float	stare	train	pants

 Exercise 2

1. Where had Tom alwāys drēamed of gōing?

   Tom alwāys_____

   _____.

2. After hē left school what did Tom become?

   After school hē joined thē Air Force and_____

   _____.

3. What was hē asked to join two yēars lāter?

   Two yēars lāter hē was asked_____

   _____.

4. List four things Tom learned to do.

Tom learned _____

_____.

Tom learned _____

_____.

Tom learned _____

_____.

Tom learned _____

_____.

Exercise 3

sight   _ _ _ _ _ ◯

phone   _ _ _ _ _ ◯ _ _

lucky   _ ◯ _ _ _ _ _ _ _

example   _ _ ◯ _ _

alwāys   _ _ _ ◯ _

rēason   _ _ _ ◯ _ _

fantastic ___ ___ ___ ◯ ___

whip ___ ◯ ◯ ___ ___

tēēth ___ ___ ___ ◯

Exercise 4

How would lambs
travel into space?

 In a ___ ___ ___ ___

___ ___ ___ ___

 Exercise 5

1. knēē   knife   kept   knōw

2. flare   front   flaw   flȳ

3. high   head   might   flight

4. nice   space   cut   place

5. gēar   ginger   damage   dānger

6. drēam   ēach   tēam   spread

7. girl   truck   sir   dirt

8. cape   dime   cake   pat

9. join   noise   rēach   point

10. count   star   round   ground

LESSON 50

Working Hard	1	2	3	4	5	6	7	8	9	10
Paying Attention	1	2	3	4	5	6	7	8	9	10
Following Instructions	1	2	3	4	5	6	7	8	9	10
Workbook Exercises	1	2	3	4	5	6	7	8	9	10
Fluency Checks	1	2	3	4	5	6	7	8	9	10

TOTAL POINTS: _____

LESSON 51

Exercise 1

tion _____ _____ _____

sion _____ _____ _____

Exercise 2

g	i	z	e	a	r	t	h	a	p
t	r	a	t	s	i	z	w	r	l
p	i	h	s	e	c	a	p	s	a
o	n	e	m	c	h	a	r	t	n
w	m	i	s	s	i	o	n	p	e
e	t	e	a	m	l	l	e	b	t
r	g	s	t	e	k	c	o	r	o

mission ☞
chart ☞
star ☜
spaceship ☜
rockets ☜
planet ☟
earth ☞
tēam ☞
power ☟

95

Exercise 3

1. "Wē want you to gō on a special __ __ __ __ __ __ __ ."
   (ssinomi)

2. "Wē think that there is __ __ __ __ on this planet." (flei)

3. " __ __ __ __ __ __ __ __ !" (ogdo) (klcu)

4. Thē __ __ __ __ __ __ __ (vilsre) space ship was ready.

5. It was as big as a __ __ __ __ __ . (rntai)

6. Thē rockets stopped __ __ __ __ __ __ __ __ . (rbungni)

7. Thē silver ship __ __ __ __ __ __ (rrdeao) towards

   thē planet.

8. Thē earth was __ __ __ __ (lube) and __ __ __ __ __

   (etwih) and __ __ __ __ __ __ __ __ __ __ . (ieufibatl)

9. But it too was very, very __ __ __ __ __ __ __ .

   (rfa) (ywāa)

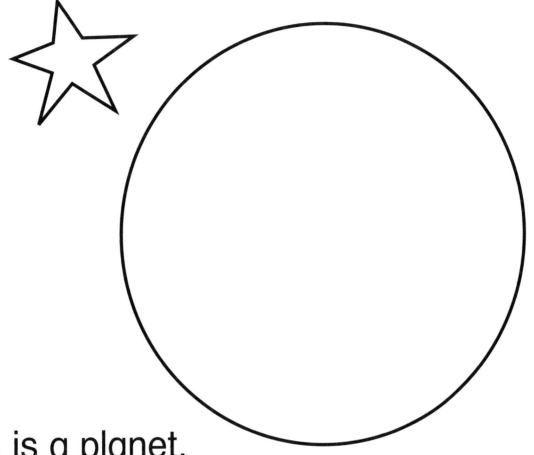

This is a planet.

Draw Tom on this planet.

Tom has special space gēar on.

Hē is holding a flag.

There is a space ship bēside Tom.

Exercise 5

_ _ _ _ _ _ _ _ _ !

LESSON 52

Exercise 1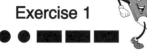

How are dogs and trēēs alike?

a	b	c	d	e	f	g	h	i	j
1	2	3	4	5	6	7	8	9	10

k	l	m	n	o	r	s	t	v	y
11	12	13	14	15	16	17	18	19	20

___ ___ ___ ___   ___ ___ ___ ___
18   8   5   20   2   15   18   8

___ ___ ___ ___   ___ ___ ___ ___ ___
 8   1   19   5   2   1   16   11   17

Exercise 2

rocket
snake
become
beautiful   voice
space   planet
stone   earth

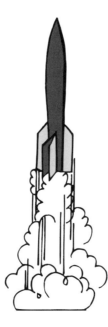

b__ __ __t__f__l

sp__c__

r__ck__t

pl__n__t

st__n__

99

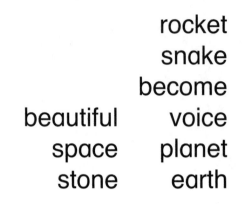

rocket
snake
become
beautiful   voice
space   planet
stone   earth

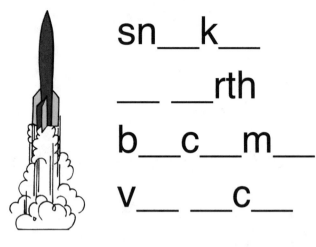

sn__k__

__ __rth

b__c__m__

v__ __c__

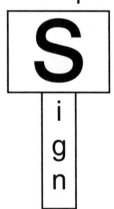

Exercise 3

Fun with Words!

Draw these words as pictures.

Example

S
i
g
n

road   roll

rocket   rope

Exercise 4

1. When they all looked out of thē space ship what did they sēē?

   They _____

   _____.

2. What did Tom put on when hē left thē silver ship?

   Tom put on _____.

3. Tom heard a voice. Where did thē voice come from?

   Thē voice _____.

4. List thrēē other things thē trēē could turn into.

   A _____

   _____

   and a huge_____ .

 **Exercise 5**

1. ☞ Tom walked around looking for_____of life.

2. ☞ "Do you mēan that you can_____into other

   things?"

3. ☞ Thē trēē turned into a _____snake.

4. ☞ "I would become a_____or water."

5. ☞ "You_____on earth kill ēach other."

6. ☞ Tom put on his_____gēar.

7. ☞ They were happy to finally land on thē small

   _____.

8. ☞ Hē heard a_____bēhind him.

9. ☞ Tom was very_____.

10. ☞ "And I alsō knōw that you are from_____."

Exercise 6

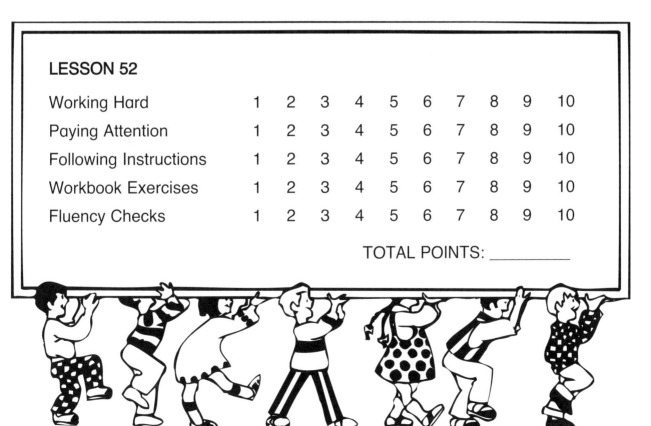

LESSON 53

Exercise 1

104

 Exercise 2

buy •	• air
break •	• door
fīnd •	• shēēt
found •	• ground
four •	• hour
mēēt •	• kīnd
power •	• mine
sign •	• moan
stone •	• shake
their •	• whȳ

 Exercise 3 <u>T</u>rue <u>F</u>alse

1._____Tom alwāys drēamed about gōing into space.

2._____After school Tom joined thē Army.

3._____Two yēars lāter Tom joined thē space tēam.

4._____Tom found thē job very ēasy. Hē had very little to do.

5._____Tom's job was to make new space ships.

6._____Thē silver space ship was as big as a train.

7._____When Tom got to thē small planet hē saw many

strānge men.

8.____Tom said that they had come to thē planet to hurt these men.

Exercise 4

1. What did thē gīant snake turn into?

    Thē gīant snake turned into_____ .

2. What did hē say to Tom?

    "
    _____

    _____ ."

3. How did thē tall man use his special power?

    Thē tall man could chānge so that_____

    _____ .

4. When would thē tall man tēach people on earth about his powers?

    Hē would tēach them his powers if_____

    _____ .

5. Whȳ could Tom and his tēam hardly wait to get home?

    They could hardly wait to get home to_____

    _____ .

6. What could make earth a better place to live?

_____

_____

  Exercise 5 Use thē letters in thē word disappēar to make eight new words.

disappēar

_____   _____   _____   _____

_____   _____   _____   _____

LESSON 53

Working Hard	1	2	3	4	5	6	7	8	9	10
Paying Attention	1	2	3	4	5	6	7	8	9	10
Following Instructions	1	2	3	4	5	6	7	8	9	10
Workbook Exercises	1	2	3	4	5	6	7	8	9	10
Fluency Checks	1	2	3	4	5	6	7	8	9	10

TOTAL POINTS: _____

LESSON 54

  Exercise 1

gīant ◯ __ ◯ __ __ __

wēēk __ __ __ __ ◯ __ __ __ __

question __ __ ◯ __ __ __ __ __

sign __ __ ◯ __ __ __ __ __

action __ __ __ __ ◯ __

beautiful __ __ __ __

thousand __ __ __ __ ◯ __ __ __

die __ __ __

fīnally __ __ ◯ __ __ __ ◯ __

lose __ __ __ __

 __ __ __ __ __ __ __ __ __ __ __ __ __ __

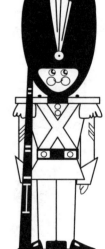

108

Exercise 2

one	strānge	planet	dance
some	phone	bother	pants
match	snake	rubber	which
mile	come	stone	wide

 Exercise 3

_____ A snake turns into a tall man.

_____ Tom becomes a pīlot.

_____ Tom mēēts a talking trēē.

_____ Tom and his crew plan to rēturn to thē planet.

_____ Tom drēams of space.

_____ Tom learns all of thē jobs of thē crew.

 Exercise  4

fi_ _	sh ch	dol_ _in	ph th
so_ _	tch ck	_ _ife	kn ph
b_ _t	ou oa	st_ _l	ou oo

109

Exercise 5

__ __ __   __ __ __ __   __ __ __ __ __

u i f   c b m e   f b h m f

Exercise 6  **Fun with Words!**

Make these words look like their meaning.

gīant   pie

river   high

110

LESSON 54

Working Hard	1	2	3	4	5	6	7	8	9	10
Paying Attention	1	2	3	4	5	6	7	8	9	10
Following Instructions	1	2	3	4	5	6	7	8	9	10
Workbook Exercises	1	2	3	4	5	6	7	8	9	10
Fluency Checks	1	2	3	4	5	6	7	8	9	10

TOTAL POINTS: _____

LESSON 55

Exercise 1

1. What were Cathy and Phil doing when they found thē cave?

   They found thē cave while_____

   _____.

2. What did Phil think it might have bēēn?

   Phil thought it looked like_____ .

3. What did Cathy think they might fīnd?

   Cathy thought they might fīnd_____.

4. How did they gō down thē mine shaft?

   They tied_____

   _____.

5. What made Cathy scrēām?

   _____ made Cathy scrēām.

6. Whȳ did Phil not gō into thē small ōpening?

   Thē ōpening was _____

   _____ for Phil.

   Hē alsō thought it could _____.

7. What did Phil hēār a short while later?

   Phil heard _____

   _____.

8. What had happened?

   Thē tunnel _____ .

112

What kind of bat doesn't have wings?

st△rtle
cr△zy
dis△ppēar
△nyone

△

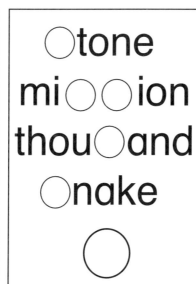
○tone
mi○○ion
thou○and
○nake

○

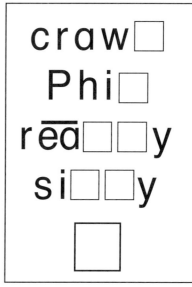
craw□
Phi□
rēa□□y
si□□y

□

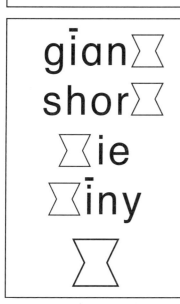
gīan⊠
shor⊠
⊠ie
⊠īny

⊠

hō◇ō
māy◇ē
◇elieve
a◇oard

◇

hik⬡
strāng⬡
car⬡ful
danc⬡

⬡

___ ___ ___ ___ ___ ___ ___ ___ ___
△   ◇   △   ○   ⬡   ◇   △   □   □

___ ___ ___
◇   △   ⊠

113

1. ōpening   bottom   phone   rope

2. face   scanned   space   cave

3. mine   tie   Phil   hike

4. disappēar   rēally   check   scrēam

5. bēgan   break   māybē   hockēy

6. island   believe   tie   sign

Exercise 4

A gold mine of words

```
c m s k i t f a h s
a i h o l e ō c g h
v n f i z p s d o p
e e x p l o r e l m
o s l d a r k c d a
t g n i n e p ō m d
q s t u n n e l a b
```

cave
explore
gold
mine
ōpening
rope
shaft
tunnel
damp
hole
dark

LESSON 55

Working Hard	1	2	3	4	5	6	7	8	9	10
Paying Attention	1	2	3	4	5	6	7	8	9	10
Following Instructions	1	2	3	4	5	6	7	8	9	10
Workbook Exercises	1	2	3	4	5	6	7	8	9	10
Fluency Checks	1	2	3	4	5	6	7	8	9	10

TOTAL POINTS: _____

LESSON 56

Exercise 1

car •	• come
friend •	• bēam
heard •	• are
mȳ •	• do
quite •	• end
scrēam •	• flȳ
some •	• ground
sound •	• mail
trail •	• sight
through •	• word

Exercise ②X **ā** and **a** sounds

What a good idea! On this grāy dāy I plan to stāy and bake cakes. I will take thē baked cakes to Jim thē jet pīlot and to Carla thē mate of thē sloop.

Exercise 3

_____ Cathy sēēs a small ōpening.

_____ Cathy and Phil tie a rope to a trēē and gō down thē

116

mine shaft.

_____ Some bats flȳ past Cathy's face and out of thē cave.

_____ Cathy and Phil gō hīking and fīnd a cave.

_____ Phil hēārs a loud crash and a scrēām.

_____ Cathy says, "I'll bē back soon," and crawls into thē tīny hole.

Exercise 4

1. List four things Phil did after hē heard thē crash and thē scrēām.

   Hē_____.

   Hē_____.

   Hē_____.

   Hē_____.

2. What did hē tell thē people in thē parking lot?

   Hē told thē people that thē tunnel _____

   _____ and that his friend was _____ .

3. How was thē man āble to call for help?

   Hē had a _____ .

4. What did thē small woman sāy had happened to Cathy?

   Shē said that Cathy had bēēn _____

   _____.

5. How did thē two firefighters fēēl after they looked into thē smaller tunnel?

_____

_____

 **Exercise 5** ● ● ■ ■ ■ ■

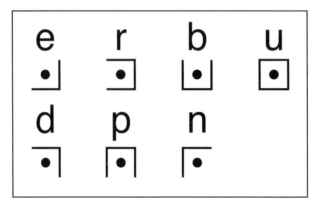 

How did thē firefighter fēēl when all his friends forgot his birthdāy?

 Hē was __ __ __ __ __ __ __ __.

Exercise 6 (on next page ☞)

road
laugh
rocket
giant
snake
firefighter
dance
dolphin
phone
pie

Across

Down

119

LESSON 57

example: old cold __bold__   ✔ bold

1. too who _____   crawl

2. tough enough _____   excite

3. small ball _____   sock

4. floor door _____   name

5. right tonight _____   pain

6. game same _____   stuff

7. contain plane _____   blue

8. walk talk _____   more

X Exercise ②

dance   crawl   ambūlance   expect

moaned   Phil   old   trȳ

rip   lie   disappēar   pain

rēally   plēase   firefighter   listen

Exercise 3

Make five new words from thē letters in

firefighter

_____ _____

_____ _____ _____

 **Exercise 4**  **T**rue **?** **F**alse

1. Phil and Cathy found an old cabin while they

   were hīking. _____

2. Cathy was startled by a flȳing bat. _____

3. Phil crawled into a small ōpening in thē cave. _____

4. Phil found some gold in thē mine shaft. _____

5. Phil ran to thē parking lot for some help. _____

6. A small woman went in thē tunnel to help Cathy. _____

7. Thē small woman said shē thought Cathy had

   brōken her arm. _____

8. Four firefighters came down thē rope. _____

Exercise 5

1. Where was Cathy?

   Cathy lāy very still_____

   _____.

2. When Cathy moved her leg, what did thē pain make

   her do?

   _____

3. What did thē small woman sāy to Cathy?

   Thē woman said, "_____."

4. Who was āble to get Cathy out of thē mine?

   _____

   _____

5. How long did it take for her leg to hēal?

   It took_____for her leg to hēal.

6. What good lesson did Cathy learn?

   _____

   _____

ē and e sounds

Now Ēdith and Frēd want cak<u>e</u>. Tom th<u>ē</u> space man and th<u>ē</u> monst<u>e</u>r want som<u>e</u> too. I think that māyb<u>ē</u> P<u>e</u>te and his j<u>e</u>t black cat can s<u>e</u>ll cak<u>e</u>s to th<u>e</u>m.

Exercise 7

laugh	a	e	__ __ __a__ __e
special	m	c	m__c__
much	b	n	b__n__ __ __ __ __ __ __
number	u	a	__ __u__ __a__ __
become	l	l	__ __ __ll
strānge	a	u	__au__ __
still	n	b	n__ __b__ __
mountain	c	m	__ __c__m__
binocūlars	e	a	__ __e__ __a__

LESSON 57

Working Hard	1	2	3	4	5	6	7	8	9	10
Paying Attention	1	2	3	4	5	6	7	8	9	10
Following Instructions	1	2	3	4	5	6	7	8	9	10
Workbook Exercises	1	2	3	4	5	6	7	8	9	10
Fluency Checks	1	2	3	4	5	6	7	8	9	10

TOTAL POINTS: _____

LESSON 58

Exercise ① OX ī and ĭ sounds

I̱ di̱d bake fi̱ve fi̱ne cakes last wēēk. I̱n nō ti̱me they were as thi̱n as a di̱me and a mi̱le wi̱de. They looked like fi̱ve i̱slands. Thi̱s i̱s not ni̱ce! Now I̱ have fi̱ve fi̱ne di̱me cakes.

Exercise 2

knock   br<u>ead</u>   h<u>igh</u>   r<u>ēa</u>lly   sm<u>all</u>   ac<u>tion</u>

kn<u>ō</u>w   h<u>ead</u>   fl<u>igh</u>t   g<u>ēa</u>r   <u>a</u>lw<u>ā</u>ys   mi<u>ssion</u>

  Exercise 3

Sēē if you can make eight new words from thē letters in thē word

holidāys

_____   _____   _____

_____   _____   _____

Exercise 4

1. When Dan woke up hē was rēally __xc__t__d.

2. T__d__y hē turned t__n.

3. Hē noticed a g__ __nt b__x with a big silver balloon on top.

4. Thē box h__d n__t b__ __n th__r__ th__ n__ght b__f__r__.

5. Dan fl__w ōver to thē box like a r__ck__t.

6. Dan couldn't b__l__ __v__ his __y__s.

7. Dan felt like a m__n of __ct__ __n, a m__n with a m__ss__ __n, a m__n with a pl__n.

Exercise 5

1. How old was Dan that dāy?

_____

2. What did Dan notice that got his attention?
   Dan noticed _____

   _____.

3. Whȳ was Dan puzzled?

_____

4. Why could Dan not believe his eyes?

_____

_____

_____

5. List four things that were inside the box.

_____   _____

_____   _____

landed   _ _ O _ _ _ _ _

excited   _ _ _ O _ _ _

mattress   O _ _ _ _ _ O _

ripped   _ _ _ O _ _

waited   _ _ _ O _ _ _

ambūlance   _ _ _ O

started   _ _ _ _ _ _ _

holidāys   _ _ O _ _ _ _

pair   _ _ _ _

his   _ _ _ _ _ _ _

127

Exercise 7

START →

Here is Dan's birthdāy gift. Sēē how fast you can get into it and out of it!

↘ FINISH

LESSON 58

Working Hard	1	2	3	4	5	6	7	8	9	10
Paying Attention	1	2	3	4	5	6	7	8	9	10
Following Instructions	1	2	3	4	5	6	7	8	9	10
Workbook Exercises	1	2	3	4	5	6	7	8	9	10
Fluency Checks	1	2	3	4	5	6	7	8	9	10

TOTAL POINTS: _____

LESSON 59

Exercise 1

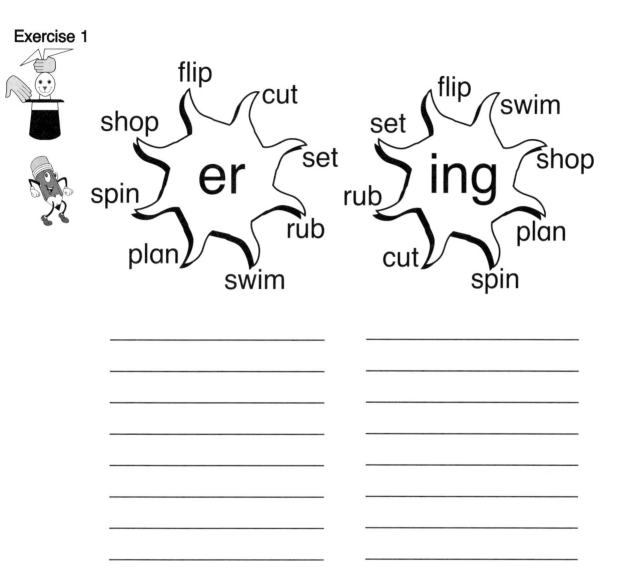

er: flip, cut, shop, set, spin, rub, plan, swim

ing: flip, swim, set, shop, rub, plan, cut, spin

_____   _____
_____   _____
_____   _____
_____   _____
_____   _____
_____   _____
_____   _____
_____   _____

Exercise ② OX   **Ō and O sounds**

I t<u>oo</u>k a ph<u>ō</u>t<u>ō</u>graph <u>of</u> thē five <u>o</u>dd cakes.

Then I put thē cakes in a b<u>o</u>x. I t<u>oo</u>k them t<u>o</u> thē <u>o</u>cean

which is thē h<u>o</u>me <u>of</u> thē sēā m<u>o</u>nster. But I was at thē

wr<u>o</u>ng p<u>o</u>nd. Hē was l<u>o</u>ng g<u>o</u>ne. A strānge h<u>ō</u>b<u>ō</u> came ōver. Hē ōpened thē bōx. Hē ate thē cakes on top. In nō time all thē cakes were gone.

? **Exercise 3**

g l e r o h s b t e a
m t t a o b h g g r c
f l o a t a i r n z a
m f h d o l p h i n p
u t k g c n w p b a t
w a t e r l r t b o a
r d t m n a e c o g i
i s l a n d c a b r n
s s a g t k k i t s s

ocean ☞
island ☞
dolphin ☞
shipwreck ☜
boat ☞
captain ☜
shore ☞
water ☞
bobbing ☝
float ☞

 Exercise 4 # <u>T</u>rue <u>F</u>alse

_____ 1. Dan was turning ten.

_____ 2. When Dan woke up hē noticed a small box with a red ribbon on it.

_____ 3. When Dan shook thē box it made a noise.

_____ 4. Inside thē box was a gīant puzzle and some toys.

_____ 5. Dan was rēally excīted about thē summer holidāys.

Exercise 5

1. What two things was Dan ēagerly waiting for?

_____

_____

2. Where did Dan and his father put up thē tent?

_____

_____

3. Whȳ did Dan put thē fake snake at thē door of his tent?

_____

_____

4. What stēēred Dan to thē shore of a strānge island?

_____

_____

5. What could thē captain sēē from his plane?

_____

_____

6. What did Dan's pārents sāy that made him excīted?

_____

_____

_____

LESSON 60

Exercise 1

Sēē if you can make eight new words
from thē letters in

adventure

_____   _____   _____   _____

_____   _____   _____   _____

Exercise ②X   **Ū** and **U** sounds

Mȳ drēam sēēms sō true! I will tell it. I drēamed
that throu̱gh mȳ binocū̱lars I saw a cu̱te cu̱b come ou̱t of a
tu̱nnel in thē mou̱ntain. Hē was fu̱ll of fu̱n and had soft fu̱r.
Hē qu̱ickly moved sou̱th u̱ntil hē came u̱pon a silver slu̱g
in a cu̱be. Hē held thē cu̱be u̱p and gave it a tu̱g. Then I
woke u̱p.

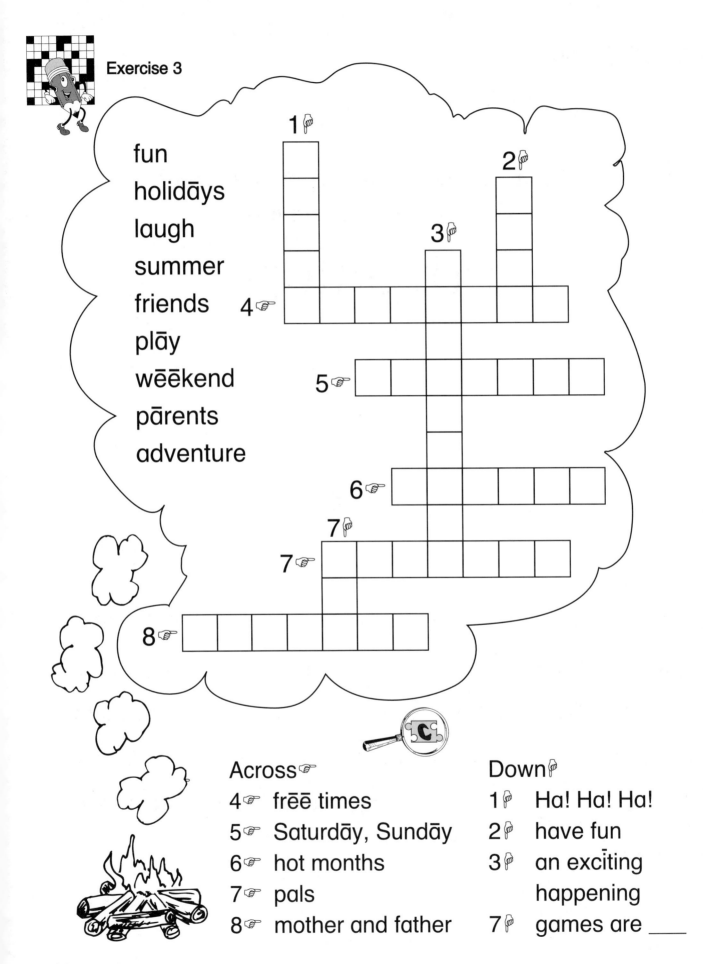

fun
holidāys
laugh
summer
friends
plāy
wēēkend
pārents
adventure

Across
4 frēē times
5 Saturdāy, Sundāy
6 hot months
7 pals
8 mother and father

Down
1 Ha! Ha! Ha!
2 have fun
3 an excīting happening
7 games are ___

Exercise 4

_____ Dan shook thē box. Hē listened. There was nō sound.

_____ Dan and his father put up thē tent in thē back yard.

_____ Dan woke up excīted on his birthdāy.

_____ Dan's pārents said hē could invite two friends ōver for thē wēēkend.

_____ Inside thē box was a full set of camping gēar.

_____ Dan spent hours in and around his tent.

_____ Dan noticed a gīant box with a big silver balloon on top.

Exercise 5

1. How did Matt and Jordan fēēl about thē adventure?

_____

_____

2. What did thē boys have for dinner?

_____

_____

3. List four things thē boys did bēfore drifting off to slēēp?

_____

_____

_____

_____

4. What woke Dan up?

_____

5. What did Jordan think thē noise was?

Jordan thought thē noise was just _____.

6. Whȳ did thē boys' eyes grōw as big as dinner plates?

Bēcause suddenly there was_____.

7. What sent thē boys flȳing out of thē tent and into thē house?

_____ sent thē boys

flȳing out of thē tent.

8. What was thē midnight monster?

_____

_____

Exercise 6

There is a small fire close to thē tent.

Dan is standing nēār thē fire.

Hē is holding a stick with a hot dog on it.

Hē has his binocūlars around his neck.

There is a trash can bēhind thē tent.

A raccoon is nēar thē trash can.

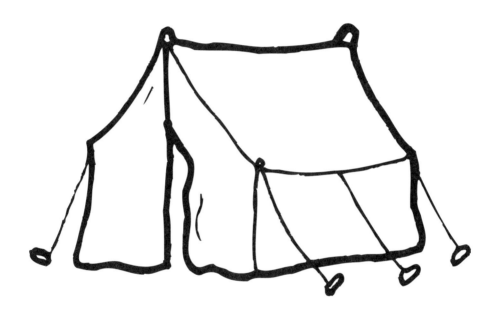

Sound Fluency Chart

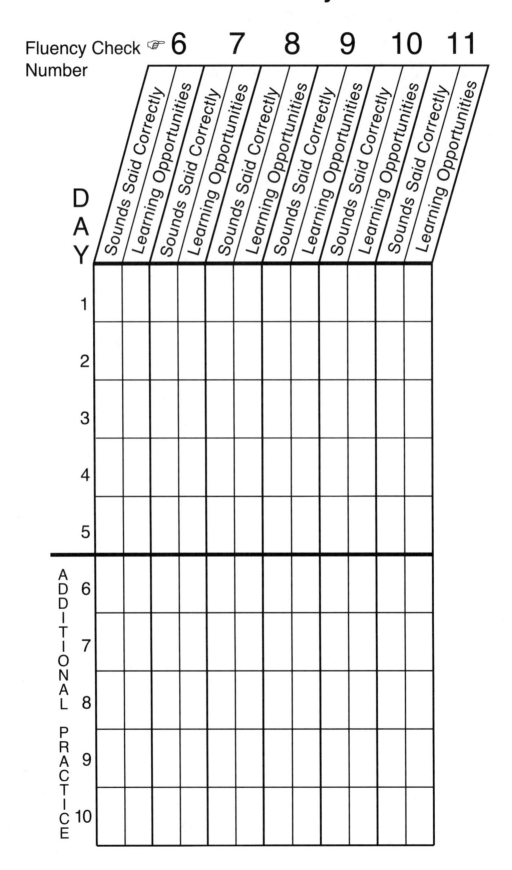

Fluency Check Number ☞ 6 7 8 9 10 11

DAY	6 Sounds Said Correctly	6 Learning Opportunities	7 Sounds Said Correctly	7 Learning Opportunities	8 Sounds Said Correctly	8 Learning Opportunities	9 Sounds Said Correctly	9 Learning Opportunities	10 Sounds Said Correctly	10 Learning Opportunities	11 Sounds Said Correctly	11 Learning Opportunities
1												
2												
3												
4												
5												
ADDITIONAL PRACTICE 6												
7												
8												
9												
10												

Word Fluency Chart

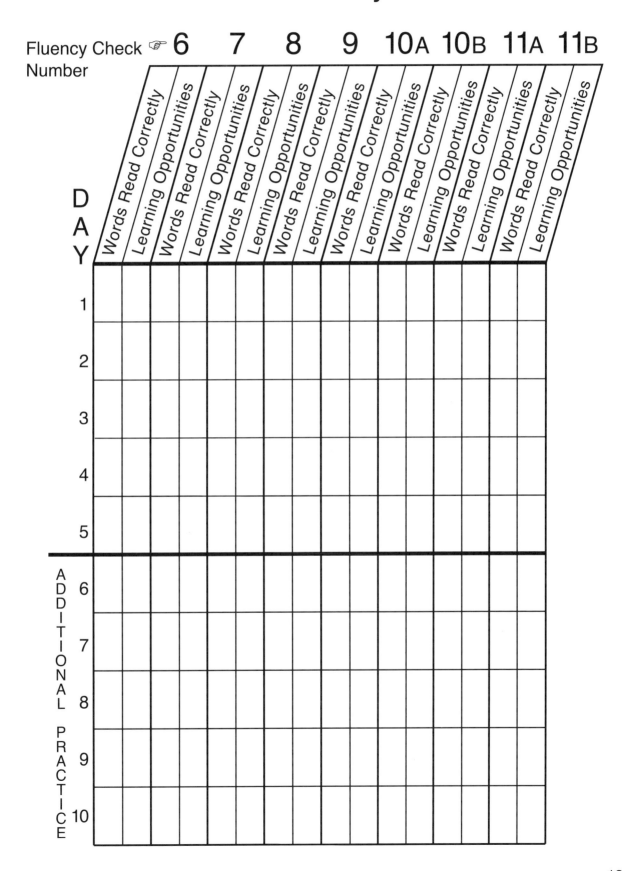

Fluency Check Number ☞	6		7		8		9		10A		10B		11A		11B	
DAY	Words Read Correctly	Learning Opportunities	Words Read Correctly	Learning Opportunities	Words Read Correctly	Learning Opportunities	Words Read Correctly	Learning Opportunities	Words Read Correctly	Learning Opportunities	Words Read Correctly	Learning Opportunities	Words Read Correctly	Learning Opportunities	Words Read Correctly	Learning Opportunities
1																
2																
3																
4																
5																
ADDITIONAL PRACTICE 6																
7																
8																
9																
10																

Story Reading Fluency Chart

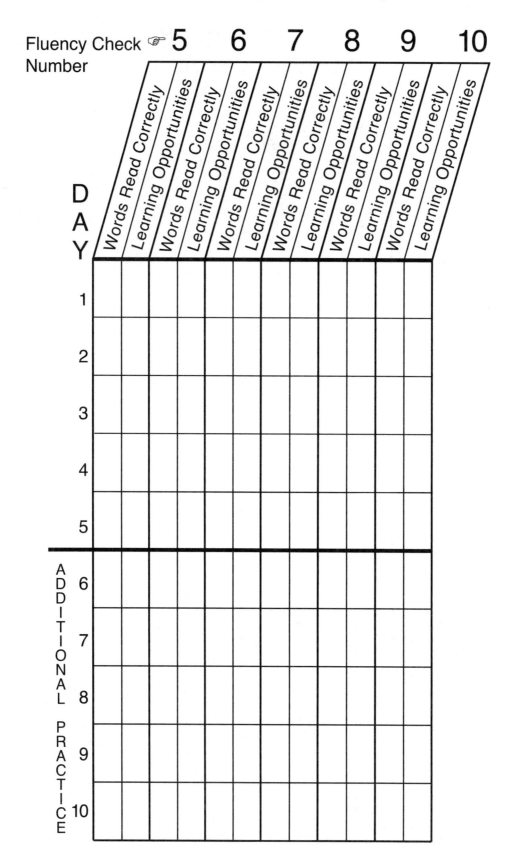

Points Chart ~ Lessons 31 - 60

LESSON	Points Earned	Running Total	Points Spent	Balance	LESSON	Points Earned	Running Total	Points Spent	Balance
31					46				
32					47				
33					48				
34					49				
35					50				
36					51				
37					52				
38					53				
39					54				
40					55				
41					56				
42					57				
43					58				
44					59				
45					60				